50 Mini Dessert: Big Flavor Recipes for Home

By: Kelly Johnson

Table of Contents

- Mini Cheesecakes
- Chocolate Mousse Cups
- Tartlets with Fresh Fruit
- Mini Panna Cottas
- Cookie Dough Bites
- Lemon Curd Tartlets
- Brownie Bites
- Raspberry Macarons
- Mini Eclairs
- Fruit Sorbet Cups
- Chocolate-Covered Strawberries
- Mini Tiramisu
- Cupcake Bites
- Key Lime Pie Jars
- Mini Pavlovas
- Almond Joy Truffles
- No-Bake Peanut Butter Bars
- Mini Red Velvet Cakes
- Matcha Green Tea Cupcakes
- S'mores Cups
- Coconut Cream Pie Bites
- Mini Crème Brûlées
- Chocolate Chip Cookie Cups
- Mini Fruit Galettes
- Mocha Pots de Crème
- Berry Parfaits
- Mini Fruit Pizzas
- Pistachio Baklava Bites
- Mini Whoopie Pies
- Chocolate Dipped Oreos
- Mini Apple Crumbles
- Caramel Flan Bites
- Strawberry Shortcake Cups
- Mini Pumpkin Pies
- Chocolate Chip Blondies

- Mini Cheesecake Pops
- Lemon Meringue Tarts
- Mini Cinnamon Rolls
- Nutella Stuffed Dates
- Mini Chocolate Tarts
- Orange Olive Oil Cake Bites
- Mini Banana Bread Loaves
- Salted Caramel Cupcakes
- Mini Coconut Macaroons
- Mini Chocolate Lava Cakes
- Berry Almond Crumble Bites
- Mini Pies (various flavors)
- Churro Bites
- Mini Scones with Jam
- Chocolate Peanut Butter Fudge

Mini Cheesecakes

Ingredients:

- 1 cup graham cracker crumbs
- 1/4 cup sugar
- 1/2 cup butter, melted
- 16 oz cream cheese, softened
- 1/2 cup sugar
- 1 tsp vanilla extract
- 2 eggs

Instructions:

1. Preheat the oven to 325°F (160°C).
2. In a bowl, mix graham cracker crumbs, 1/4 cup sugar, and melted butter; press into the bottom of mini muffin tins.
3. In another bowl, beat cream cheese, 1/2 cup sugar, and vanilla until smooth. Add eggs one at a time, mixing well.
4. Pour the cream cheese mixture over the crusts and bake for 15-20 minutes.
5. Let cool, then refrigerate for at least 2 hours before serving.

Chocolate Mousse Cups

Ingredients:

- 6 oz dark chocolate, chopped
- 2 tbsp butter
- 2 eggs, separated
- 1/4 cup sugar
- 1 cup heavy cream

Instructions:

1. Melt chocolate and butter in a double boiler or microwave; let cool slightly.
2. In a bowl, whisk egg yolks with sugar until pale. Add melted chocolate and mix.
3. In another bowl, beat egg whites until stiff peaks form. Fold into the chocolate mixture.
4. In a separate bowl, whip heavy cream until soft peaks form; fold into the chocolate mixture.
5. Spoon into cups and refrigerate for at least 2 hours before serving.

Tartlets with Fresh Fruit

Ingredients:

- 1 package pre-made tartlet shells
- 1 cup pastry cream (store-bought or homemade)
- Fresh fruit (berries, kiwi, mango, etc.)
- Apricot jam, for glaze

Instructions:

1. Fill each tartlet shell with pastry cream.
2. Arrange fresh fruit on top of the cream.
3. Heat apricot jam until melted and brush over the fruit for a glaze.

Mini Panna Cottas

Ingredients:

- 1 cup heavy cream
- 1/4 cup sugar
- 1 tsp vanilla extract
- 1/2 tsp gelatin
- 2 tbsp cold water

Instructions:

1. In a small bowl, sprinkle gelatin over cold water and let sit for 5 minutes.
2. In a saucepan, heat cream and sugar until dissolved. Remove from heat and stir in gelatin and vanilla.
3. Pour into mini cups and refrigerate for at least 4 hours until set.

Cookie Dough Bites

Ingredients:

- 1/2 cup butter, softened
- 1/2 cup brown sugar
- 1/4 cup granulated sugar
- 1 tsp vanilla extract
- 1 cup flour (heat-treated)
- 1/2 cup mini chocolate chips

Instructions:

1. In a bowl, cream together butter, brown sugar, and granulated sugar.
2. Mix in vanilla and flour until combined. Stir in chocolate chips.
3. Roll into small balls and refrigerate until firm.

Lemon Curd Tartlets

Ingredients:

- 1 package pre-made tartlet shells
- 1 cup lemon curd (store-bought or homemade)
- Fresh berries for garnish

Instructions:

1. Fill each tartlet shell with lemon curd.
2. Top with fresh berries before serving.

Brownie Bites

Ingredients:

- 1/2 cup butter
- 1 cup sugar
- 2 eggs
- 1 tsp vanilla extract
- 1/3 cup cocoa powder
- 1/2 cup flour
- 1/4 tsp salt

Instructions:

1. Preheat the oven to 350°F (175°C) and grease a mini muffin tin.
2. Melt butter and mix with sugar, eggs, and vanilla.
3. Stir in cocoa, flour, and salt until combined.
4. Fill muffin cups and bake for 10-12 minutes. Let cool before serving.

Raspberry Macarons

Ingredients:

- 1 cup powdered sugar
- 1/2 cup almond flour
- 2 egg whites
- 1/4 cup granulated sugar
- 1/2 cup raspberry jam

Instructions:

1. Preheat the oven to 300°F (150°C).
2. In a bowl, sift powdered sugar and almond flour together.
3. In another bowl, beat egg whites until soft peaks form; gradually add granulated sugar until stiff peaks form.
4. Fold dry ingredients into egg whites until combined.
5. Pipe small circles onto a baking sheet lined with parchment paper.
6. Let sit for 30 minutes to form a skin. Bake for 15-20 minutes.
7. Once cool, sandwich two macaron shells with raspberry jam.

Enjoy your delightful desserts!

Mini Eclairs

Ingredients:

- **Choux Pastry:**
    - 1/2 cup water
    - 1/4 cup butter
    - 1/2 cup all-purpose flour
    - 2 large eggs
- **Filling:**
    - 1 cup heavy cream
    - 1/4 cup powdered sugar
    - 1 tsp vanilla extract
- **Chocolate Ganache:**
    - 1/2 cup chocolate chips
    - 1/4 cup heavy cream

Instructions:

1. Preheat the oven to 400°F (200°C).
2. In a saucepan, combine water and butter; bring to a boil. Add flour and stir until a dough forms.
3. Remove from heat, cool slightly, and add eggs one at a time until fully incorporated.
4. Pipe small logs onto a baking sheet and bake for 20-25 minutes until golden.
5. For the filling, whip cream with powdered sugar and vanilla until stiff peaks form.
6. For ganache, heat cream and pour over chocolate chips; stir until smooth.
7. Once eclairs are cool, fill with whipped cream and dip tops in chocolate ganache.

Fruit Sorbet Cups

Ingredients:

- 2 cups frozen fruit (strawberries, mango, or mixed berries)
- 1/4 cup sugar (adjust to taste)
- 1/2 cup water
- Fresh fruit for garnish

Instructions:

1. In a blender, combine frozen fruit, sugar, and water; blend until smooth.
2. Pour mixture into cups and freeze for at least 2 hours.
3. Serve garnished with fresh fruit.

Chocolate-Covered Strawberries

Ingredients:

- 1 lb fresh strawberries
- 8 oz chocolate (dark, milk, or white)
- Optional toppings: crushed nuts, sprinkles

Instructions:

1. Melt chocolate in a microwave or double boiler until smooth.
2. Dip each strawberry in the melted chocolate, letting excess drip off.
3. Place on parchment paper and sprinkle with toppings if desired.
4. Refrigerate until chocolate hardens.

Mini Tiramisu

Ingredients:

- 1 cup strong brewed coffee, cooled
- 1/4 cup coffee liqueur (optional)
- 8 oz mascarpone cheese
- 1/2 cup heavy cream
- 1/4 cup sugar
- 1 package ladyfinger cookies
- Cocoa powder for dusting

Instructions:

1. In a bowl, mix coffee and liqueur.
2. In another bowl, whip cream with sugar until stiff peaks form, then fold in mascarpone.
3. Quickly dip ladyfingers in the coffee mixture and layer in small cups.
4. Add a layer of mascarpone mixture, repeat, and finish with mascarpone on top.
5. Dust with cocoa powder and refrigerate for at least 2 hours before serving.

Cupcake Bites

Ingredients:

- 1 box cake mix (any flavor)
- 1 cup frosting (store-bought or homemade)
- Chocolate or candy coating for dipping

Instructions:

1. Bake cake according to package instructions; let cool completely.
2. Crumble the cake into a bowl and mix in frosting until combined.
3. Roll into small balls and refrigerate until firm.
4. Dip each ball in melted chocolate or candy coating and place on parchment paper.
5. Let set before serving.

Key Lime Pie Jars

Ingredients:

- **Crust:**
    - 1 cup graham cracker crumbs
    - 1/4 cup butter, melted
- **Filling:**
    - 1 can (14 oz) sweetened condensed milk
    - 1/2 cup key lime juice
    - 3 large egg yolks
- **Topping:**
    - Whipped cream

Instructions:

1. In a bowl, mix graham cracker crumbs and melted butter; press into the bottom of jars.
2. In another bowl, whisk together sweetened condensed milk, key lime juice, and egg yolks.
3. Pour filling over the crust in jars.
4. Bake at 350°F (175°C) for about 15 minutes. Let cool, then refrigerate.
5. Top with whipped cream before serving.

Mini Pavlovas

Ingredients:

- 2 large egg whites
- 1/2 cup granulated sugar
- 1/4 tsp vinegar
- 1/4 tsp cornstarch
- Whipped cream and fresh fruit for topping

Instructions:

1. Preheat the oven to 225°F (110°C).
2. Whip egg whites until soft peaks form; gradually add sugar and beat until stiff peaks form.
3. Fold in vinegar and cornstarch.
4. Pipe or spoon small mounds onto a baking sheet lined with parchment paper.
5. Bake for 1 hour, then turn off the oven and let cool completely.
6. Top with whipped cream and fresh fruit before serving.

Almond Joy Truffles

Ingredients:

- 1 cup shredded coconut
- 1/4 cup almond butter
- 1/4 cup powdered sugar
- 1/4 cup chopped almonds
- 8 oz dark chocolate, for coating

Instructions:

1. In a bowl, mix shredded coconut, almond butter, powdered sugar, and chopped almonds until combined.
2. Roll into small balls and refrigerate until firm.
3. Melt dark chocolate and dip each ball, placing them on parchment paper.
4. Let set in the refrigerator before serving.

Enjoy making these delicious mini desserts!

No-Bake Peanut Butter Bars

Ingredients:

- 1 cup graham cracker crumbs
- 1 cup creamy peanut butter
- 1/2 cup powdered sugar
- 1/2 cup chocolate chips (for topping)

Instructions:

1. In a bowl, mix graham cracker crumbs, peanut butter, and powdered sugar until well combined.
2. Press the mixture into an 8x8-inch baking pan lined with parchment paper.
3. Melt chocolate chips and spread over the peanut butter layer.
4. Refrigerate for at least 2 hours until firm. Cut into bars and serve.

Mini Red Velvet Cakes

Ingredients:

- 1 box red velvet cake mix
- Ingredients listed on cake mix box (usually eggs, oil, and water)
- Cream cheese frosting (store-bought or homemade)

Instructions:

1. Preheat the oven to 350°F (175°C) and prepare a mini cupcake pan with liners.
2. Prepare the red velvet cake batter according to the box instructions.
3. Fill each mini cupcake liner about two-thirds full and bake for 10-12 minutes.
4. Let cool, then frost with cream cheese frosting.

Matcha Green Tea Cupcakes

Ingredients:

- 1 cup all-purpose flour
- 1 tsp baking powder
- 1/4 tsp salt
- 1/2 cup sugar
- 1/4 cup unsalted butter, softened
- 1 large egg
- 1/2 cup milk
- 1-2 tsp matcha powder (adjust for desired color)

Instructions:

1. Preheat the oven to 350°F (175°C) and line a mini cupcake pan with liners.
2. In a bowl, mix flour, baking powder, salt, and matcha powder.
3. In another bowl, cream butter and sugar until fluffy. Add egg and milk; mix well.
4. Gradually combine wet and dry ingredients.
5. Fill mini cupcake liners and bake for 10-12 minutes. Let cool before serving.

S'mores Cups

Ingredients:

- 1 cup graham cracker crumbs
- 1/4 cup sugar
- 1/4 cup butter, melted
- 1 cup mini marshmallows
- 1 cup chocolate chips

Instructions:

1. Preheat the oven to 350°F (175°C).
2. Mix graham cracker crumbs, sugar, and melted butter; press into the bottom of a mini muffin tin.
3. Bake for 5-7 minutes.
4. Remove from oven and add chocolate chips and mini marshmallows on top.
5. Bake for an additional 2-3 minutes until marshmallows are golden. Let cool before removing from the tin.

Coconut Cream Pie Bites

Ingredients:

- 1 cup shredded coconut
- 1/2 cup cream cheese, softened
- 1/4 cup powdered sugar
- 1/4 cup coconut cream
- Mini graham cracker crusts

Instructions:

1. In a bowl, mix cream cheese, powdered sugar, and coconut cream until smooth.
2. Stir in shredded coconut.
3. Spoon the mixture into mini graham cracker crusts and refrigerate for at least 1 hour before serving.

Mini Crème Brûlées

Ingredients:

- 1 cup heavy cream
- 1/4 cup sugar
- 1/2 tsp vanilla extract
- 2 egg yolks
- Extra sugar for caramelizing

Instructions:

1. Preheat the oven to 325°F (160°C).
2. In a saucepan, heat cream and sugar until dissolved; remove from heat and stir in vanilla.
3. In a bowl, whisk egg yolks, then gradually add the cream mixture.
4. Pour into mini ramekins and place them in a baking dish with hot water.
5. Bake for 30-35 minutes until set. Cool and refrigerate. Before serving, sprinkle sugar on top and caramelize with a kitchen torch.

Chocolate Chip Cookie Cups

Ingredients:

- 1 cup cookie dough (store-bought or homemade)
- Mini chocolate chips (optional)

Instructions:

1. Preheat the oven to 350°F (175°C).
2. Grease a mini muffin tin and press a small amount of cookie dough into each cup, making a well in the center.
3. Bake for 10-12 minutes until golden.
4. Let cool slightly, then add mini chocolate chips in the center. Allow to cool completely before removing.

Mini Fruit Galettes

Ingredients:

- 1 sheet pie crust (store-bought or homemade)
- 1 cup mixed fresh fruit (berries, peaches, etc.)
- 2 tbsp sugar
- 1 tbsp cornstarch
- 1 egg (for egg wash)

Instructions:

1. Preheat the oven to 375°F (190°C).
2. Roll out the pie crust and cut into small circles.
3. In a bowl, mix fresh fruit, sugar, and cornstarch.
4. Place a spoonful of the fruit mixture in the center of each dough circle. Fold the edges over the fruit, leaving the center exposed.
5. Brush edges with beaten egg and bake for 20-25 minutes until golden.

Enjoy creating these delightful mini desserts!

Mocha Pots de Crème

Ingredients:

- 1 cup heavy cream
- 1/2 cup milk
- 1/4 cup sugar
- 2 oz dark chocolate, chopped
- 2 large egg yolks
- 1 tsp instant coffee or espresso powder
- 1/2 tsp vanilla extract

Instructions:

1. Preheat the oven to 325°F (160°C).
2. In a saucepan, heat cream, milk, sugar, and coffee powder until just simmering. Remove from heat and stir in chocolate until melted.
3. In a bowl, whisk egg yolks, then gradually add the chocolate mixture. Stir in vanilla.
4. Pour into small ramekins and place in a baking dish with hot water.
5. Bake for 25-30 minutes until set. Cool, then refrigerate for at least 2 hours before serving.

Berry Parfaits

Ingredients:

- 2 cups mixed berries (strawberries, blueberries, raspberries)
- 1 cup Greek yogurt
- 1/4 cup honey or maple syrup
- Granola for layering

Instructions:

1. In a bowl, mix yogurt and honey until smooth.
2. In cups or jars, layer yogurt, berries, and granola.
3. Repeat layers until jars are filled. Serve immediately or refrigerate until serving.

Mini Fruit Pizzas

Ingredients:

- 1 package sugar cookie dough (store-bought or homemade)
- 1 cup cream cheese, softened
- 1/4 cup powdered sugar
- Assorted fresh fruit (kiwi, strawberries, blueberries)

Instructions:

1. Preheat the oven according to cookie dough instructions.
2. Roll out and cut cookie dough into small rounds. Bake until golden and let cool.
3. In a bowl, mix cream cheese and powdered sugar until smooth.
4. Spread cream cheese mixture over cooled cookie rounds and top with assorted fresh fruit.

Pistachio Baklava Bites

Ingredients:

- 1 package phyllo dough
- 1 cup chopped pistachios
- 1/2 cup butter, melted
- 1/4 cup sugar
- 1/4 tsp cinnamon
- 1/2 cup honey
- 1/4 cup water

Instructions:

1. Preheat the oven to 350°F (175°C).
2. In a bowl, mix pistachios, sugar, and cinnamon.
3. Layer phyllo dough in a mini muffin tin, brushing each layer with melted butter.
4. Place a spoonful of the pistachio mixture in each cup and top with more phyllo layers.
5. Bake for 15-20 minutes until golden.
6. In a saucepan, heat honey and water until combined; drizzle over baked baklava bites.

Mini Whoopie Pies

Ingredients:

- **Cookies:**
    - 1 cup all-purpose flour
    - 1/2 cup cocoa powder
    - 1 tsp baking powder
    - 1/4 tsp salt
    - 1/2 cup butter, softened
    - 1 cup sugar
    - 1 large egg
    - 1 tsp vanilla extract
- **Filling:**
    - 1/2 cup marshmallow fluff
    - 1/4 cup cream cheese, softened
    - 1/4 cup powdered sugar

Instructions:

1. Preheat the oven to 350°F (175°C).
2. In a bowl, mix flour, cocoa powder, baking powder, and salt.
3. In another bowl, cream butter and sugar until fluffy. Add egg and vanilla; mix well.
4. Gradually add dry ingredients to the wet mixture.
5. Drop spoonfuls onto a baking sheet and bake for 10-12 minutes. Let cool.
6. For filling, mix marshmallow fluff, cream cheese, and powdered sugar until smooth.
7. Sandwich filling between two cookies to form whoopie pies.

Chocolate Dipped Oreos

Ingredients:

- 1 package Oreo cookies
- 8 oz chocolate (dark, milk, or white)
- Sprinkles or chopped nuts (optional)

Instructions:

1. Melt chocolate in a microwave or double boiler until smooth.
2. Dip each Oreo in chocolate, letting excess drip off.
3. Place on parchment paper and sprinkle with toppings if desired.
4. Refrigerate until chocolate hardens.

Mini Apple Crumbles

Ingredients:

- 2 apples, peeled and diced
- 1/4 cup brown sugar
- 1/2 tsp cinnamon
- 1/4 cup oats
- 1/4 cup flour
- 1/4 cup butter, melted

Instructions:

1. Preheat the oven to 350°F (175°C).
2. In a bowl, mix diced apples, brown sugar, and cinnamon.
3. In another bowl, mix oats, flour, and melted butter until crumbly.
4. Divide apple mixture into mini ramekins and top with crumble mixture.
5. Bake for 20-25 minutes until golden and bubbly.

Caramel Flan Bites

Ingredients:

- 1/2 cup sugar (for caramel)
- 1 can (14 oz) sweetened condensed milk
- 1 can (12 oz) evaporated milk
- 3 large eggs
- 1 tsp vanilla extract

Instructions:

1. In a saucepan, heat sugar until melted and caramelized; pour into mini ramekins to coat the bottom.
2. In a blender, combine condensed milk, evaporated milk, eggs, and vanilla; blend until smooth.
3. Pour the mixture over the caramel in ramekins.
4. Place ramekins in a baking dish with hot water and bake at 350°F (175°C) for 40-45 minutes until set.
5. Cool, then refrigerate before serving.

Enjoy creating these delicious mini desserts!

Strawberry Shortcake Cups

Ingredients:

- 2 cups strawberries, sliced
- 2 tbsp sugar
- 1 cup heavy cream
- 2 tbsp powdered sugar
- 1 tsp vanilla extract
- 1 cup pound cake, cubed

Instructions:

1. In a bowl, toss strawberries with sugar and let sit for 15 minutes.
2. In another bowl, whip heavy cream with powdered sugar and vanilla until soft peaks form.
3. In serving cups, layer pound cake cubes, whipped cream, and macerated strawberries.
4. Repeat layers and serve immediately.

Mini Pumpkin Pies

Ingredients:

- 1 cup pumpkin puree
- 1/2 cup sweetened condensed milk
- 1/4 cup sugar
- 1/2 tsp cinnamon
- 1/4 tsp nutmeg
- 1/4 tsp ginger
- 1 package mini pie crusts

Instructions:

1. Preheat the oven to 350°F (175°C).
2. In a bowl, mix pumpkin puree, condensed milk, sugar, and spices until smooth.
3. Pour mixture into mini pie crusts.
4. Bake for 15-20 minutes until set. Let cool before serving.

Chocolate Chip Blondies

Ingredients:

- 1/2 cup butter, melted
- 1 cup brown sugar
- 1/4 cup sugar
- 1 egg
- 1 tsp vanilla extract
- 1 1/2 cups flour
- 1/2 tsp baking powder
- 1/2 cup chocolate chips

Instructions:

1. Preheat the oven to 350°F (175°C) and grease a mini muffin tin.
2. In a bowl, mix melted butter, brown sugar, and white sugar until smooth.
3. Add egg and vanilla; mix well.
4. Gradually add flour and baking powder, then fold in chocolate chips.
5. Spoon batter into mini muffin tins and bake for 12-15 minutes. Let cool before serving.

Mini Cheesecake Pops

Ingredients:

- 8 oz cream cheese, softened
- 1/2 cup powdered sugar
- 1 tsp vanilla extract
- 1 cup graham cracker crumbs
- 1/4 cup melted butter
- Lollipop sticks
- Chocolate for coating

Instructions:

1. In a bowl, mix cream cheese, powdered sugar, and vanilla until smooth.
2. Form into small balls and freeze for 1 hour.
3. Mix graham cracker crumbs with melted butter; set aside.
4. Dip frozen cheesecake balls in melted chocolate and then roll in graham cracker mixture.
5. Insert lollipop sticks and refrigerate until set.

Lemon Meringue Tarts

Ingredients:

- **Crust:**
    - 1 cup graham cracker crumbs
    - 1/4 cup sugar
    - 1/4 cup butter, melted
- **Filling:**
    - 1/2 cup lemon juice
    - 1/4 cup sugar
    - 2 egg yolks
    - 1/2 cup water
- **Meringue:**
    - 2 egg whites
    - 1/4 tsp cream of tartar
    - 1/4 cup sugar

Instructions:

1. Preheat the oven to 350°F (175°C).
2. Mix crust ingredients and press into mini tart pans. Bake for 10 minutes.
3. In a saucepan, whisk lemon juice, sugar, egg yolks, and water; cook until thickened.
4. Pour filling into tart crusts.
5. For meringue, beat egg whites and cream of tartar until soft peaks form; gradually add sugar until stiff peaks form.
6. Spread meringue over filling and bake for 5-7 minutes until golden.

Mini Cinnamon Rolls

Ingredients:

- 1 can refrigerated crescent roll dough
- 1/4 cup butter, softened
- 1/4 cup brown sugar
- 1 tbsp cinnamon
- Cream cheese frosting for drizzling

Instructions:

1. Preheat the oven according to crescent roll instructions.
2. Unroll dough and spread with softened butter. Sprinkle with brown sugar and cinnamon.
3. Roll up tightly and cut into small pieces.
4. Bake according to package instructions until golden. Drizzle with cream cheese frosting before serving.

Nutella Stuffed Dates

Ingredients:

- 12 Medjool dates, pitted
- 1/2 cup Nutella
- Chopped nuts or sea salt for topping (optional)

Instructions:

1. Slice each date lengthwise, but not all the way through.
2. Fill each date with a spoonful of Nutella.
3. Top with chopped nuts or a sprinkle of sea salt if desired. Serve immediately or refrigerate until ready to serve.

Mini Chocolate Tarts

Ingredients:

- **Crust:**
    - 1 cup chocolate cookie crumbs
    - 1/4 cup butter, melted
- **Filling:**
    - 1 cup heavy cream
    - 8 oz chocolate, chopped
    - 1 tsp vanilla extract

Instructions:

1. Preheat the oven to 350°F (175°C).
2. Mix cookie crumbs and melted butter; press into mini tart pans. Bake for 5-7 minutes.
3. In a saucepan, heat cream until simmering; pour over chopped chocolate. Stir until smooth and add vanilla.
4. Pour chocolate filling into cooled tart crusts and refrigerate until set.

Enjoy making and sharing these delightful mini desserts!

Orange Olive Oil Cake Bites

Ingredients:

- 1 1/2 cups all-purpose flour
- 1 cup sugar
- 1/2 cup olive oil
- 1 cup orange juice (freshly squeezed)
- Zest of 1 orange
- 2 large eggs
- 2 tsp baking powder
- 1/2 tsp salt

Instructions:

1. Preheat the oven to 350°F (175°C) and grease a mini muffin tin.
2. In a bowl, whisk together flour, sugar, baking powder, and salt.
3. In another bowl, mix olive oil, orange juice, zest, and eggs until well combined.
4. Combine wet and dry ingredients, mixing until just combined.
5. Fill each muffin cup about two-thirds full and bake for 15-20 minutes, or until a toothpick comes out clean. Let cool before serving.

Mini Banana Bread Loaves

Ingredients:

- 2 ripe bananas, mashed
- 1/3 cup melted butter
- 1/2 cup sugar
- 1 egg, beaten
- 1 tsp vanilla extract
- 1 tsp baking soda
- Pinch of salt
- 1 cup all-purpose flour

Instructions:

1. Preheat the oven to 350°F (175°C) and grease mini loaf pans.
2. In a bowl, mix mashed bananas with melted butter.
3. Stir in sugar, beaten egg, and vanilla.
4. Add baking soda and salt, then mix in flour until just combined.
5. Divide batter among the mini loaf pans and bake for 20-25 minutes. Let cool before serving.

Salted Caramel Cupcakes

Ingredients:

- **Cupcakes:**
    - 1 1/2 cups all-purpose flour
    - 1 cup sugar
    - 1/2 cup butter, softened
    - 2 large eggs
    - 1/2 cup milk
    - 1 1/2 tsp baking powder
    - 1/2 tsp salt
- **Salted Caramel Sauce:**
    - 1 cup sugar
    - 6 tbsp butter
    - 1/2 cup heavy cream
    - 1/2 tsp sea salt

Instructions:

1. Preheat the oven to 350°F (175°C) and line a mini cupcake pan with liners.
2. For the cupcakes, cream butter and sugar until fluffy. Add eggs, milk, baking powder, and salt; mix until combined.
3. Fill cupcake liners about two-thirds full and bake for 12-15 minutes. Let cool.
4. For the caramel sauce, heat sugar in a saucepan until melted and golden. Stir in butter until melted, then add heavy cream and sea salt.
5. Once cupcakes are cooled, drizzle with salted caramel sauce.

Mini Coconut Macaroons

Ingredients:

- 2 2/3 cups shredded coconut
- 1/2 cup sweetened condensed milk
- 1 tsp vanilla extract
- 2 egg whites
- Pinch of salt

Instructions:

1. Preheat the oven to 325°F (165°C) and line a baking sheet with parchment paper.
2. In a bowl, mix shredded coconut, sweetened condensed milk, vanilla, and salt.
3. In another bowl, beat egg whites until stiff peaks form.
4. Gently fold the egg whites into the coconut mixture.
5. Drop spoonfuls onto the prepared baking sheet and bake for 20-25 minutes until golden. Let cool before serving.

Mini Chocolate Lava Cakes

Ingredients:

- 1/2 cup butter
- 1 cup chocolate chips
- 1 cup powdered sugar
- 2 large eggs
- 2 egg yolks
- 1 tsp vanilla extract
- 1/2 cup flour

Instructions:

1. Preheat the oven to 425°F (220°C) and grease mini ramekins.
2. In a saucepan, melt butter and chocolate chips over low heat.
3. Remove from heat and stir in powdered sugar until combined.
4. Add eggs, egg yolks, and vanilla; mix well.
5. Gently fold in flour until just combined.
6. Divide batter among ramekins and bake for 12-14 minutes. Let cool for 1 minute before inverting onto plates.

Berry Almond Crumble Bites

Ingredients:

- **Filling:**
    - 1 cup mixed berries (fresh or frozen)
    - 2 tbsp sugar
    - 1 tbsp cornstarch
- **Crumble:**
    - 1/2 cup almond flour
    - 1/4 cup oats
    - 1/4 cup brown sugar
    - 1/4 cup butter, melted

Instructions:

1. Preheat the oven to 350°F (175°C) and grease a mini muffin tin.
2. In a bowl, mix berries, sugar, and cornstarch; set aside.
3. In another bowl, mix almond flour, oats, brown sugar, and melted butter until crumbly.
4. Press a spoonful of crumble mixture into each muffin cup, add a spoonful of berry filling, and top with more crumble.
5. Bake for 15-20 minutes until golden. Let cool before serving.

Mini Pies (Various Flavors)

Ingredients:

- **Crust:**
    - 1 package refrigerated pie crusts
- **Fillings:**
    - 1 cup fruit filling (apple, cherry, or blueberry) or chocolate pudding

Instructions:

1. Preheat the oven to 375°F (190°C).
2. Roll out pie crust and cut into circles to fit mini muffin tins.
3. Press circles into the muffin tin and fill with your chosen filling.
4. Top with another pie crust circle, sealing edges.
5. Bake for 20-25 minutes until golden brown. Let cool before serving.

Churro Bites

Ingredients:

- 1 cup water
- 1/2 cup butter
- 1 cup flour
- 1/4 tsp salt
- 2 large eggs
- 1/2 cup sugar
- 1 tsp cinnamon
- Oil for frying

Instructions:

1. In a saucepan, bring water and butter to a boil. Add flour and salt, stirring until it forms a ball.
2. Remove from heat and stir in eggs one at a time until smooth.
3. Heat oil in a deep pan to 350°F (175°C).
4. Pipe small bites of dough into hot oil and fry until golden brown.
5. In a bowl, mix sugar and cinnamon; roll churro bites in the mixture before serving.

Enjoy making these delightful mini desserts!

Mini Scones with Jam

Ingredients:

- 2 cups all-purpose flour
- 1/3 cup sugar
- 1 tbsp baking powder
- 1/2 tsp salt
- 1/2 cup cold butter, cubed
- 1/2 cup heavy cream
- 1 large egg
- 1 tsp vanilla extract
- Jam for serving

Instructions:

1. Preheat the oven to 400°F (200°C) and line a baking sheet with parchment paper.
2. In a large bowl, mix flour, sugar, baking powder, and salt.
3. Cut in cold butter until the mixture resembles coarse crumbs.
4. In a separate bowl, whisk together heavy cream, egg, and vanilla.
5. Add the wet ingredients to the dry ingredients, mixing until just combined.
6. Turn the dough onto a floured surface and gently knead a few times. Pat into a 1-inch thick circle and cut into wedges or use a round cutter.
7. Place on the baking sheet and bake for 15-18 minutes until golden. Let cool slightly and serve with jam.

Chocolate Peanut Butter Fudge

Ingredients:

- 1 cup chocolate chips (dark or milk chocolate)
- 1/2 cup creamy peanut butter
- 1/4 cup sweetened condensed milk
- 1/2 tsp vanilla extract

Instructions:

1. Line an 8x8-inch pan with parchment paper.
2. In a microwave-safe bowl, combine chocolate chips, peanut butter, and sweetened condensed milk.
3. Microwave in 30-second intervals, stirring after each, until melted and smooth.
4. Stir in vanilla extract.
5. Pour the mixture into the prepared pan and spread evenly.
6. Refrigerate for at least 2 hours or until set. Cut into small squares before serving.

Enjoy your mini scones and chocolate peanut butter fudge!

www.ingramcontent.com/pod-product-compliance
Lightning Source LLC
LaVergne TN
LVHW081342060526
838201LV00055B/2801